Fabulous Flutes

by Kristi Holl

Did you know that people have been playing the flute for over 40,000 years? For all this time, people around the world have loved the sound of flutes.

A flute is a **woodwind** instrument. The player makes music by blowing air over an opening. Some flutes are played by holding the flute out in front of the body and blowing one end. Others are played by holding the flute sideways and blowing air over a hole.

People have enjoyed playing and listening to flutes for many years.

Flutes developed **independently** around the world. Here are examples from Europe, North and South America, and Asia.

Flutes From Europe

The oldest-known musical instruments ever found were flutes. Flutes that are more than 40,000 years old were discovered in a cave in Germany.

The metal flute usually played in concerts today comes from Germany. A German flutist, or flute player, designed and built his own flutes in the 1800s. The flutes quickly became popular and were the **model** for the metal concert flute.

A side-blown concert flute

Flutes From North and South America

Pan flutes were played in South America thousands of years ago. Pan flutes have five or more different tubes, called pipes. Each pipe is a different length and makes a different sound. Pan flutes spread to North America, where they are used by many different Native American groups.

Pan flute

Another flute from South America is the *tarka*. These flutes are cut from a solid block of wood and have carvings of llamas, birds, and faces. They make a sound as **raspy** as desert air.

Flutes From Asia

Many flutes from Asia are made of bamboo. This kind of grass has a hollow stem. One type of bamboo flute is the *bansuri* from India. This flute is blown from the side. It has a whistling sound.

Bansuri flute

Flutes come from all around the world. They are often made of different materials, which helps give the flute its own unique sound.

Kind of Flute	Country of Origin	Made From What Materials?	Sound
Concert Flute	Germany	Metal	Sweet and airy
Pan Flute	Peru and U.S.	Reeds, cane, bird quills, bones	Light and airy
Tarka	South American countries	Wood	Raspy
Bansuri	India	Bamboo	Whistling

There are many kinds of flutes, and they come in all shapes, sizes, and sounds. Flutes are sure to be enjoyed for many years to come.

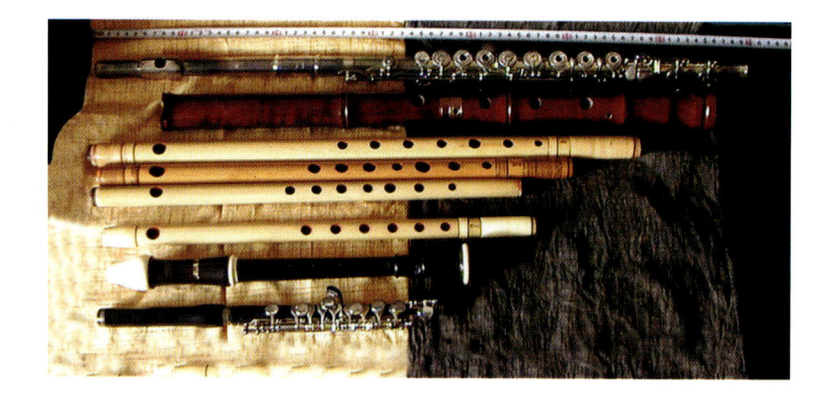